MY PET

Rats & Mice

Honor Head

Photographs by Jane Burton

Belitha Press

First published in the UK in 2000 by
Belitha Press
A member of Chrysalis Books plc
64 Brewery Road, London N7 9NT

Paperback edition first published in 2003.

ISBN 1 84138 113 6 (hardback)
ISBN 1 84138 358 9 (paperback)

British Library Cataloguing in Publication
Data for this book is available from the
British Library.

Series editor: Claire Edwards
Editor: Jinny Johnson
Designer: Rosamund Saunders
Illustrator: Pauline Bayne
Consultant: Frazer Swift

Printed in Hong Kong

10 9 8 7 6 5 4 3 2 1 (hb)
10 9 8 7 6 5 4 3 2 1 (pb)

PDSA (People's Dispensary for Sick
Animals) is Britain's largest charity which
each year provides free treatment for some
1.4 million sick and injured animals of
disadvantaged owners.

A royalty of 2.5 per cent of the proceeds
from this book will be paid to the PDSA
(People's Dispensary for Sick Animals) on
every copy sold in the UK.

The products featured have been kindly
donated by Pets at Home.

Contents

My mouse

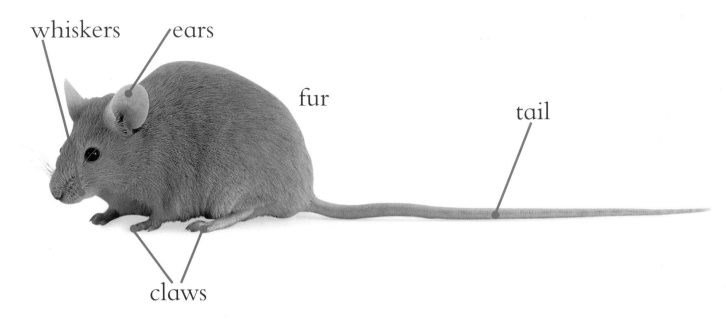

whiskers

ears

fur

tail

claws

My rat

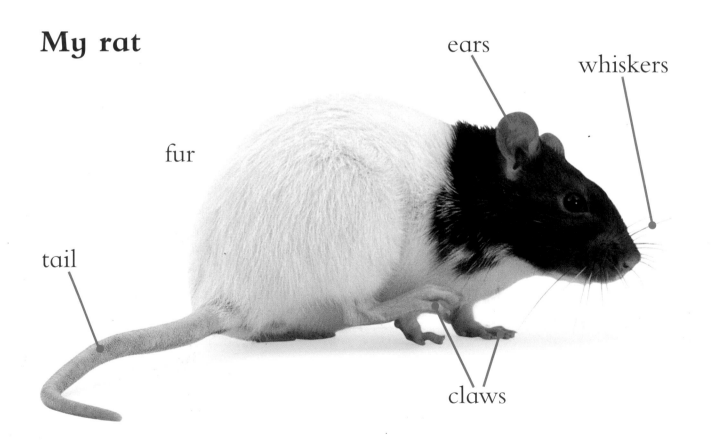

ears

whiskers

fur

tail

claws

It's fun owning your own pet.

Rats and mice are fun to own, but they need to be looked after carefully. Pet rats and mice have to be fed every day and their home should be cleaned regularly. They need plenty of exercise, too, and should be handled daily.

Young children with pets should always be supervised by an adult. For further notes, please see page 32.

What is a mouse?

Mice are part of the rodent family. They have a long tail and whiskers and they make squeaking noises. You should keep more than one mouse as they like company.

Mice are all the same shape, but they come in lots of different colours.

Some mice are the same
colour all over. Others
have stripes and
patches on
their fur.

Some mice have long fur,
but mice do not have
fur on their feet,
tail or ears.

What is a rat?

Rats are also rodents.
They are bigger
than mice and have
longer tails.

A rat's fur should be sleek
and glossy, with
no bare patches.

Rats come in different colours such as brown, silver and yellow. There are also albino rats, which are all white and have pink eyes. Some rats have spots and stripes on their fur.

In the wild, rats live in big groups. You should always keep two or more pet rats together otherwise they will get lonely.

Rats and mice build nests for their babies.

Rats and mice prepare a nest for their babies. Make sure a pregnant female is well fed and has fresh water. She will need extra paper bedding, too, for making her nest.

Baby mice and rats are born without any fur and they cannot see or hear. Do not handle the babies for the first two weeks.

Rats can have as many as 16 babies. Mice may have up to 12, but they usually have litters of about eight. The babies are ready to leave their mother when they are five to six weeks old.

Separate males and females when they are about five weeks old. If they are left together they may have babies.

Make your pets a cosy home.

Your pets can live in a cage or a glass tank. A tank is the best home for a mouse. Make sure the tank or cage is large enough for your pet, especially if you are keeping two or more together.

Prepare your pets' home by covering the floor with wood shavings. Always buy the wood shavings from a pet shop. Never use sawdust in your pets' home.

Your pets will also need a cosy nest box to sleep in. Fill this with shredded paper bedding material from a pet shop.

Do not keep rats and mice together in the same cage or tank.

Make sure your pets are comfortable.

Check that the tank or cage does not have any plastic or wooden bits that your pets can chew. Make sure all the corners are smooth so that your pets cannot hurt themselves.

Give your pets plenty to chew on. This will help to make sure their teeth do not grow too long. You can buy special blocks of wood at the pet shop for rats and mice to chew.

Mice and rats will be lonely if they are kept on their own. Keep females together. Males may fight. Don't put males and females in together as they will have lots of unwanted babies.

A carrying container is useful when taking pets to the vet. You can also use it to keep pets safe when you clean out their home.

Your pets need lots of exercise.

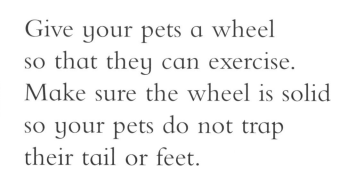

Give your pets a wheel
so that they can exercise.
Make sure the wheel is solid
so your pets do not trap
their tail or feet.

Rats and mice are good
climbers and enjoy
having a ladder or
climbing frame
they can run up
and down. A cube
with holes in
each side is fun
for them to
climb through.

Give your pets lots of objects to play with. Try making a maze of bricks for them to explore. Do not give them toys made of soft plastic.

A simple cardboard tube makes an ideal toy for your pet rats and mice.

Your pets like to play.

Your pets will need to
exercise outside the cage,
but never let them run
around the house by
themselves. Always stay
with your pets and make
sure they are safe.

Your pets will enjoy playing with you. They like to run up and down your arm and sit on your shoulder. The more often you handle your rats, the friendlier they will become.

Rats have a good sense of balance and can climb along a rope hung in their cage.

Your pets love to explore. But watch them carefully or they will chew any objects they find.

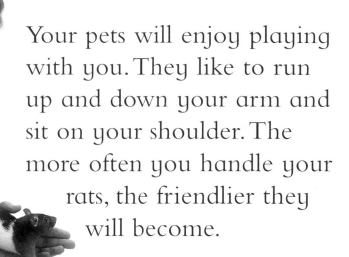

Give your pets fresh food every day.

Every day give your pets
a bowl of food bought from
the pet shop or vet. Put the
food in a heavy bowl so that
your pets do not knock it over.

**Foods such
as hard-
boiled eggs
and monkey
nuts make
delicious
treats for
your
pets.**

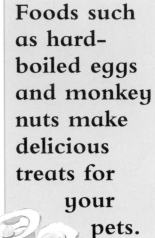

Your pets will not drink very much, but make sure they always have a drip-feeder bottle full of fresh water.

Rats and mice enjoy fresh foods two or three times a week. Give them oats or millet, greens, carrots and wholemeal bread. Wash fruit and vegetables well. Do not feed your pets lettuce.

Keep your pets' cage clean.

It is important to keep your pets' home clean. This will keep them healthy and stop them smelling. Clean out any old food and droppings every day. Wash the food bowl and make sure the water bottle is clean.

Once a week, clean out your pets' nesting box. Throw out the old stuff and put in some clean bedding material. Always wash your hands after cleaning your pets' home.

Mice and rats keep their fur very clean. They lick themselves all over several times a day.

Once a month, give your pets' home a thorough clean. Wash the cage or tank, toys, water bottle and food bowls.

Make sure everything is dry before you put in fresh bedding and wood shavings.

23

Handle your pets gently.

When you first take your pets home they will be frightened. Leave them alone in their new home for a day and night before you touch them. Then put your hand in the tank and let your pets smell your fingers. Talk gently so they learn to recognize your voice.

Be very gentle when you pick up your pet mouse. Scoop it on to the palm of your hand. Never squeeze or hold it round the middle. Keep your pet away from your face.

Never pick up your rat or mouse by its tail. Always stroke them from the head to the tail.

To hold your pet rat, place a hand around its shoulders and support its hind quarters. Your rats will like being picked up and stroked and you should do this at least twice a day.

Help your pets stay healthy.

If your pet falls to the floor, pick it up gently and check to make sure it has no broken bones. Put it back in its home and do not touch it for at least a day and night.

If it is not moving around as normal within 24 hours, take it to the vet.

If your pet gets plenty of exercise its claws shouldn't grow too long. Check the claws regularly and if they are too long, ask the vet to clip them for you.

If you do have to take your mouse or rat to the vet, make sure that it has plenty of its usual bedding to keep it warm.

Your pets should breathe easily without making a lot of noise. If your pets wheeze or snuffle, it's a good idea to take them to the vet.

Make sure your pets are safe.

You can leave your pets alone for one or two days. Check they have enough dry food. Don't leave fresh food as it will go off.

If you are going away for longer than two days, ask a friend to look after your pets while you are away.

Make sure your pets have plenty of fresh water if you need to leave them for a day or two.

Mice usually live for two to three years and rats for three or four years. If you care for them properly they will have a happy life.

But, just like people, one day they will die. This will make you feel sad but soon you will remember how much fun you had with your pets.

Words to remember

albino An animal with all white fur and pink eyes.

bedding Shredded paper you can buy from a pet shop for use in your pets' nest box.

litter A number of young born to a rat or mouse or other animal.

rodent The group of animals to which rats and mice belong.

tank A glass container that can be used to house a rat or mouse. The lid should be close-fitting and allow plenty of air into the tank.

vet An animal doctor.

whiskers Long fine hairs that grow on an animal's face.

wood shavings Specially prepared shavings used on the floor of the cage or tank. Buy these from a pet shop.

Rats grow quickly.

Newborn rats are tiny and hairless.

By 16 days a baby rat has a furry coat.

Index

Notes for parents

Rats and mice will give you and your family great pleasure, but they do need care and attention. If you decide to buy rats or mice for your child, you will need to ensure that the animals are healthy, happy and safe. You will also have to check that they have food and water, look after them if they are ill and supervise your child with the pets until he or she is at least seven years old. Rats and mice are ideal first pets, but make sure your child learns to handle the animals correctly and does not harm them.

Here are some other points to think about before you decide to own rats or mice:

- Mice live for two or three years, rats for up to four years, and they will cost money to feed and house. If your pets become ill, there may be vet's bills.

- Do you have time to feed and clean your pets regularly and to play with them so that they don't get bored and lonely?

- Do you have other pets such as dogs or cats which might frighten the rodents?

- You need somewhere to keep the rats or mice indoors. A cage or tank for two or three mice should measure at least 45 x 30 x 25 centimetres. A cage for two rats should measure at least 75 x 65 x 30 centimetres.

- Pet rats and mice are generally good tempered. Remember, though, that they do have sharp teeth and may bite if scared.

- It is best to have two rats or mice together. Two females will get on well but two males may fight, even if they are brothers. Do not keep a male and female together as they will have frequent large litters.

- If you go on holiday, make sure someone can care for your pets while you are away.

This book is intended as an introduction only for young readers. If you have any queries about how to look after your mouse or rat, you can contact the PDSA (People's Dispensary for Sick Animals) at Whitechapel Way, Priorslee, Telford, Shropshire TF2 9PQ. Tel: 01952 290999.